Ten P
about F

ex libris

Candlestick Press

Published by:

Candlestick Press,
Diversity House, 72 Nottingham Road, Arnold, Nottingham NG5 6LF
www.candlestickpress.co.uk

Design and typesetting by Craig Twigg

Printed by Ratcliff & Roper Print Group, Nottinghamshire, UK

Selection © Jonathan Edwards, Di Slaney and Katharine Towers, 2022

Introduction © Jonathan Edwards, 2022

Cover illustration © Sophie Bass, 2022
https://sophiebassillustration.bigcartel.com/

Candlestick Press monogram © Barbara Shaw, 2008

© Candlestick Press, 2022

ISBN 978 1 913627 18 8

Acknowledgements

The poems in this pamphlet are reprinted from the following books, all by
permission of the publishers listed unless stated otherwise. Every effort has been
made to trace the copyright holders of the poems published in this book. The
editor and publisher apologise if any material has been included without
permission or without the appropriate acknowledgement, and would be glad to be
told of anyone who has not been consulted.

Thanks are due to all the copyright holders cited below for their kind permission:

Fleur Adcock, *Poems 1960-2000* (Bloodaxe Books, 2000) www.bloodaxebooks.
com. Jeanette Burton, poem first published in this anthology, by kind permission
of the author. Jonathan Edwards, *My Family & Other Superheroes* (Seren Books,
2014) by kind permission of the author. Jackie Kay, *Darling: New & Selected
Poems* (Bloodaxe Books, 2007) www.bloodaxebooks.com. Vanessa Lampert, *On
Long Loan* (Live Canon, 2020) by kind permission of the author. John
McCullough, poem first published in this anthology, by kind permission of the
author. Sinéad Morrissey, *On Balance* (Carcanet Press Ltd, 2017). Cathy Stern,
The Paris Review, issue no. 135 (Summer 1995) by kind permission of the author.
R. S. Thomas, *Collected Poems: 1945-1990* (Weindenfeld & Nicholson, 2000) by
permission of Orion Books. Marvin Thomson, *Road Trip* (Peepal Tree Press,
2020) © Marvin Thompson.

All permissions cleared courtesy of Suzanne Fairless-Aitken
c/o Swift Permissions swiftpermissions@gmail.com

Where poets are no longer living, their dates are given.

Introduction

Families, huh? What can we do with them? They make us laugh, make us cry, break our hearts, bring us joy. There's no escaping their hugs and their accents, their eccentricities, their love. How can poems conjure words to celebrate the daft magic of family?

For RS Thomas, the family gives us some amazing things, and a number of these poems explore the wonder of these gifts. In Sinéad Morrissey's 'My Life According to You,' a mother's life-story is re-imagined by an admiring daughter, while in Vanessa Lampert's 'Sand,' a grandfather makes a car out of sand for a little girl, who magically takes it "out for a spin".

The family can connect us to history, in all sorts of interesting ways. Marvin Thompson considers how history can be passed onto the next generation, while in Cathy Stern's poem, the response to looking at a family photo from the past is so strong that the speaker "want[s] to enter the picture, slip myself / into 1903." John McCullough's 'Family' gives us a Christmas gathering of "queer ghosts," featuring Dusty Springfield, Algernon Swinburne and Roland Barthes.

Family is a great subject for comedy, and you'll find all sorts of humour in these pages, from the sibling rivalry in Fleur Adcock's poem, to the image of a baby at the top of a human pyramid, reaching for a star. But it is also from the family that we draw all that's important: our values, our sense of identity and our sense of love. Jeanette Burton offers us an unforgettable origins story, while Jackie Kay gives us the emotional experience of an adoptive mother.

If you were to take a character from each of these poems, you might end up with an extraordinary, fantastical group. But would it really be any more strange or wonderful than our actual families? Each family is the same in how completely wonderful it is, and here are ten poems to raise a glass and a cheer, to sing loudly of all the joy of families.

Jonathan Edwards

Gifts

From my father my strong heart,
My weak stomach.
From my mother the fear.

From my sad country the shame.

To my wife all I have
Saving only the love
That is not mine to give.

To my one son the hunger.

RS Thomas (1913 – 2000)

My Life According To You

So I was born and was small for ages
and then suddenly a cardboard box
appeared with two furry black ears
sticking out of it it made me nervous
but I was brave and gave it a bell
to play with and then out it jumped
and loved me it was my cat I called it
Morris Morrissey it matched
my mother's Morris Minor

                                     For the next bit

I was a teenager and then I grew up
I had a flat in Dublin and a boyfriend
he was a vet little bed little kitchen
little towel rack lots of little cups
and saucers and then off he went
to Africa he sent me pictures
of giraffes and of the second
tallest waterfall in the world
when he got back he wasn't my friend

                                       anymore I cried

for a week I was also at university
a bigger place than school with bigger
chairs and desks and when it finished
I found a suitcase it was red
with purple flowers it had a scarf
around the handle I put in everything
I needed socks and a jotter and snacks
and took a plane across the ocean
to Japan to visit Godzilla

                                       where it was

summer and boiling hot and the people
all kept wind chimes to make it
cooler and rode bicycles to the shops
and at the same time held up umbrellas
though it wasn't even raining
and when I met a man in a bright
white classroom the darkest parts
of our eyes turned into swirls then question
marks then hearts so we got married

                        and went hippety

hoppety splat a mountain a lake
a desert we bought a house a tiny one
at first and then a massive one a baby
knocked at the door one night
but didn't come in and then another
baby came he cried a lot
we thought he had tummy ache
we gave him a bath in a bucket
he was just lonely

                        for his sister

to come and keep him company
but you were still floating about
in space inside your bubble egg
it had accessories a switch
for going sideways a switch
for going upside down or faster
it was a cross between a sparkly green
and a sparkly silver the moon
was very annoying and then whenever

                        we'd all been bored

on our own for long enough down
you came on a path of lightning
to finish off the family you were born
on the living room floor at three
in the morning in front of the trampoline-
sofa and I heard them say *A Girl!*
and sat up straightaway we were both
pretty and I opened out my arms
and that's it really

When you grow up

I'm going to be so busy taking you
to the house shop waiting by the play-
ground gates to bring your children
swimming I won't be any different
I'll keep your room exactly as it is
for you to visit bric-a-brac collection
on the shelf the bed your father built
the letters of your name in neon
appearing on the ceiling

when it's time

Sinéad Morrissey

Sand

On Woolacombe beach my Grandpa builds
an MG convertible sports car from sand,
in front of the swingboats where I was sick once.

My car faces the wind-ruffled sea, roof down
under a sky made from torn strips of paper.
Grandpa slowly carves the bonnet and makes me

a member of the AA. He shapes the wheels
and stands back, proud as a car salesman.
Other kids are staring. They want to be me.

In a few weeks my parents will separate,
but now our orange windbreak holds them
close together in flowery beach chairs

safe from the wind. I sit behind the steering wheel
of my new MG. The engine starts first try.
I take her out for a spin to Lundy Island

to see the puffins and the granite stacks
and back, beeping my horn to warn the surfers,
who wave. I park her where she was before,

facing out to sea. Mum looks up from her book
and says *it must be time for a 99.*
I want to jump on my car before we leave,

and ruin her so no one else can ruin her,
but Grandpa won't let me. He takes my hand
in his, saying *don't look back. Let's go.*

Vanessa Lampert

Family

Oh God, who invited them? The queer ghosts
are here, rock up, unfixable, each Christmas—
hell-bent relatives. No prezzies.
Each just brings catastrophes and wonky ideas.
Dusty loiters under mistletoe like a purple smell
while Roland cracks his quip about the laundry truck,
Radclyffe complains to brandy butter.
Only cheesecakes understand me...

Can't they leave us alone? Don't they understand
there's a finite number of times you can listen
to a 500 year old essayist reminisce
about a paper cut, watch Katherine disappear
up a ladder of lies or Algernon's bloodless rump
on the banister, avalanching toward you?

There's no arranging them like tinsel.
You cannot seat Langston next to Virgil
and his pet fly, paper hats for all.
Bothering is part of it, with the greats
as much as the nameless crowd outside
who flank my windows, nosing at glass,
their bodies packed tightly as snow.

John McCullough

The Video

When Laura was born, Ceri watched.
They all gathered around Mum's bed –
Dad and the midwife and Mum's sister
and Ceri. 'Move over a bit,' Dad said –
he was trying to focus the camcorder
on Mum's legs and the baby's head.

After she had a little sister,
and Mum had gone back to being thin,
and was twice as busy, Ceri played
the video again and again.
She watched Laura come out, and then,
in reverse, she made her go back in.

Fleur Adcock

My brother's latest theory on why there are no baby photos of me

is delivered in the style of a Poirot murder mystery.
My family gathered together in the back garden
one Sunday afternoon after a BBQ.
My mum has brought out a smorgasbord
of baby photos, but, as usual, none are of me.
Just snaps of my brother, his rolls of fat
packed into a nappy and romper suit.
His mop of white-blonde curls brings gasps
of delight from my niece and nephew,
who have only ever known him with brown hair,
a few flecks of grey running through it.

My mother is captured on these photos too,
always leaning forward, but with her head tilted
towards the camera. She has hold of my brother's
outstretched arms and in various scenes from childhood,
toddles him past caravans, along beaches, lifts him
out of rubber dinghies, on to bikes with stabilisers.
My dad looks at a few, says to me, *Well, it could be you.*
It's hard to tell. You both looked the same as babies.
My mum shakes her head, confirms her son's identity
with a long, convoluted calculation of dates,
clothing, car models, the weather.

And so to the theory: my brother holds the floor,
various expectant faces looking up at him
from sun loungers and deck chairs.
I put it to you, he postulates, *that this woman*
(pointing at me) *is, in fact, an imposter.*
The rest of the story goes that as a five-year old
orphan I was abandoned on *his* parents' drive,
lots were drawn by the neighbours
and *his* mother and father drew the short straw.

We all laugh, apart from my mum, who disappears
inside the house on a mission to locate one solitary
photograph of her fabled baby daughter.

In her absence, my brother entertains us all
with his previous hypotheses:
the day we watched *Back to the Future*
and he somehow managed to convince me
that, like Marty and the McFly siblings,
I was slowly being erased from existence.
Then there was my 16th birthday party
where he revealed my criminal connections
to a group of shy teenagers huddled together
around the buffet table, nibbling on the fluffy
wings of fairy cakes, sipping on Buck's Fizz.
Oh yes! Her real folks are Mexican drug lords!

An hour later, my mother returns to the garden,
waving the valuable piece of evidence in her hand.
It's a photograph of my christening.
Finally, there I am, wrapped in so much white wool
I look like a tiny sheep in my father's arms.
My mother is resplendent in a tangerine suit,
hair permed and dyed a matching auburn.
The other participants are a roll call
of half-remembered neighbours,
godparents, one set of grandparents.

But wait. Hang on. There is no sign of my brother.
No little boy peering out from behind his dad's legs.
Me again! First-born son christened at St Peter's!
My mother comes to the rescue, all eyes on her now.
This tale goes that my brother threw a tantrum,

refused to be on the photo, hid behind a tree.
Theory disproved, he admits defeat, all is settled.
It's like an episode of *Surprise Surprise* now;
everyone whooping and hugging as if some long-lost
daughter had literally appeared on the back lawn.

Baby photographs safely back in the album,
family members all accounted for,
I can't help forming my own hypothesis:
one where there is no sulking, no fit of temper,
only the pretence of a paddy and hot tears.
One where my three-year-old brother hides
behind a giant oak, waits until the coast is clear,
sneaks past the adults posing for my christening photo.
He enters the church through a side door, kneels
in front of the altar, thanks God for this shiny new toy.
A glorious plaything. Something else to wind up.

Jeanette Burton

The one in which my children discuss jazz while we set out to watch *The Lego Batman Movie* in Blackwood

A crow rises into the morning mizzle as mist clings to the valley.
Tired, I bark at my five-year-old Derys to 'Focus'
on her seatbelt. She cries. I wipe mucus from her top lip

and tell her there's liquorice in my rucksack. She kicks my bag.
Hayden (aged six) shouts, 'This music's angry!'
On alto sax, Joe Harriott's abstract jazz swirls around us.

'Sad and crazy!' snaps Derys. We fall into silence.
As I drive, a smile curls – my Mixed Race children are listening
to something I want them to love: art that sings

Africa's diaspora and raises skin to radiance.
But they haven't asked to learn a history of defiance
or the blues' dark beauty. Is this upbringing

or brainwashing? Below the grey-green hills in Hafodyrynys,
Hayden asks, 'Does the trumpet sound like a forest fire or an arrest?'
My best mate's mixtapes melted during the policing protest

that blazed on Broadwater Farm. Should we tour the bliss
and sadness those high-rises hold for me? 'Where we live's not racist,'
I was once warned. Cymbals shimmer. A loneliness rests.

Marvin Thompson

Generation

Inside the picture it is 1903 – late spring or early summer.
The three women sit on the front porch steps,
a potted fern to their right on the middle stair,
another pot of what looks like vinca higher up
on the porch itself. Delicate ivy vines fall
from the low railing; a profusion of blurred leaves
moves up the turned wooden column at the porch's edge
and disappears at the top of the picture.
The woman in the middle, sitting highest,
holds a baby of three months or more,
who wears a bright white dress and smiles.
The baby is my father, and my young grandmother,
her hair piled high and caught with a ribbon,
her high-necked, dotted-swiss dress trimmed with ruffles
and appliquéd lace, looks quietly down
on her first born, her face so beautiful
I catch my breath. Her mother sits to her left,
gray and aging at forty-eight, unfrivolous
in her tailored skirt, blouse, and jacket;
her grandmother sits to her right, plump and white-haired,
serene in gingham and a long lace collar.
I can't take my eyes from their faces, their clothes.
I want to enter the picture, slip myself
into 1903, climb into the dresses and sit on the porch,
become each woman, touch the baby,
find the unborn daughter I will be.

Cathy Stern

Chapter 3: The Waiting Lists
(from *The Adoption Papers*)

The first agency we went to
didn't want us on their lists,
we didn't live close enough to a church
nor were we church-goers
(though we kept quiet about being communists).
The second told us
we weren't high enough earners.
The third liked us
but they had a five-year waiting list.
I spent six months trying not to look
at swings nor the front of supermarket trolleys,
not to think this kid I've wanted could be five.
The fourth agency was full up.
The fifth said yes but again no babies.
Just as we were going out the door
I said oh you know we don't mind the colour.
Just like that the waiting was over.

This morning a slim manilla envelope arrives
postmarked Edinburgh: one piece of paper
I have now been able to look up your microfiche
(as this is all the records kept nowadays).
From your mother's letters, the following information:
Your mother was nineteen when she had you.
You weighed eight pounds four ounces.
She liked hockey. She worked in Aberdeen
as a waitress. She was five foot eight inches.

I thought I'd hid everything
that there wasnie wan
giveaway sign left

I put Marx Engels Lenin (no Trotsky)
in the airing cupboard – she'll no be
checking out the towels surely

All the copies of the *Daily Worker*
I shoved under the sofa
the dove of peace I took down from the loo

A poster of Paul Robeson
saying give him his passport
I took down from the kitchen

I left a bust of Burns
my detective stories
and the Complete Works of Shelley

She comes at 11.30 exactly.
I pour her coffee
from my new Hungarian set

And foolishly pray she willnae
ask its origins – honestly
this baby is going to my head.

She crosses her legs on the sofa
I fancy I hear the *Daily Workers*
rustle underneath her

Well she says, you have an interesting home
She sees my eyebrows rise.
It's different she qualifies.

Hell and I've spent all morning
trying to look ordinary
– a lovely home for the baby.

She buttons her coat all smiles
I'm thinking
I'm on the home run

But just as we get to the last post
her eye catches at the same times as mine
a red ribbon with twenty world peace badges

Clear as a hammer and sickle
on the wall.
Oh, she says are you against nuclear weapons?

To Hell with this. Baby or no baby.
Yes I says. Yes yes yes.
I'd like this baby to live in a nuclear free world.

Oh. Her eyes light up.
I'm all for peace myself she says,
and sits down for another cup of coffee.

Jackie Kay

My Family in a Human Pyramid

My uncle starts it, kneeling in his garden;
my mother gives a leg up to my gran.
When it's my turn to climb, I get a grip
of my bamp's miner's belt, my cousin's heels,
say *Thank you* for her birthday card as I go,
then bounce on my nan's perm and skip three rows,
land on my father's shoulders. He grabs my ankles,
half holding me up and half holding me close.

Here he comes, my godson, Samuel Luke,
passed up until he's standing in his nappy
on my head. And now to why we're here:
could the Edwardses together reach a height
that the youngest one of us could touch a star?
Sam reaches out. He points towards the night.

Jonathan Edwards